Contents

Introduction

More than any previous conflict, World War II involved entire populations. People living at home far from the fighting faced shortages, and whole communities were mobilised to support – and pay for – the war effort.

World War II was a highly technological conflict. It depended on the production of arms and ammunition, together with tanks, fighter aircraft, ships and submarines. From the start of the war, whichever side could produce more materiel—a word that describes all military equipment— would have an advantage.

As the war began, whole economies were converted to military production. Normal peacetime activity virtually disappeared. The military had priority for scarce resources: nylon and silk for clothes, for example, were diverted to make parachutes and military uniforms.

The resulting shortages were usually controlled by means of rationing that limited individuals to strict allocations of new goods. Food, too, was rationed increasingly throughout the war. Britain, which depended on imported food, imposed rations from early in the war; Germany and Japan, which both started the war with more generous allowances, ran dangerously short of food near its end, when they were facing defeat.

Arsenal of Democracy

In the United States, rations were relatively generous. Even before the country officially joined the war in December 1941, however, industrial production had been geared up to provide materiel for the Allies. U.S. President Franklin D. Roosevelt said that he wanted to make the United States 'the arsenal of democracy'.

Women and Children

With so many men called into military service, it was necessary to find new workers to keep industry functioning. Millions of women in all combatant countries found themselves working in factories or shipyards or on farms. For many the change was welcome: they escaped the home and enjoyed making friends with their colleagues; they had their own income for the first time. At the end of the war, when returning soldiers reclaimed their jobs, many women found it difficult to return to a role as a traditional housewife.

Changes in women's roles also impacted children. Some had their lives disrupted by being evacuated from their homes to places at less risk of bombing. Others were pressed into military service. All suffered the same shortages, dangers and upheaval to their normal lives as the rest of the population.

⇒ **This U.S. poster shows a woman working in a factory while she thinks of her husband on the battlefield. It makes a direct link between success on the front line and industrial production at home.**

⇧ Even before the United States entered the war, some Americans wanted U.S. industry to help the Allies – Britain, France and others – in Europe.

Industry

More than any previous conflict, World War II depended on industrial production. All countries involved dedicated their factories to manufacturing the goods needed for victory.

The most important products included aircraft and tanks, artillery, weapons and ammunition. But countries also needed huge numbers of ships and military vehicles, along with goods to make sure that civilians on the home front lived reasonably well.

Industry in the United States

In the United States the demands of the war finally ended the effects of the Great Depression that had begun in 1929. When the war started in Europe in September 1939, more than 15 per cent of U.S. workers were still unemployed (a normal unemployment rate today is about 5 per cent).

LIBERTY SHIPS

When German U-boats sank British cargo ships, U.S. shipyards produced thousands of vessels to replace them. These so-called liberty ships were manufactured in a process that engineer Henry Kaiser based on assembly lines in the car industry. The ships had standard parts that could be put together by workers with little experience, including many women. The speed of assembly rose quickly: by the middle of 1942 it took only 80 hours to build a ship, and three were being completed every day. The Allies were building cargo ships far quicker than the German navy could sink them. The liberty ships – 2,700 were produced in all – helped ensure that the British would not be starved into surrender.

⇧ Liberty ships near completion at a shipyard in California in 1943. The ships' panels were joined by welding, which was far quicker than riveting.

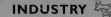

⇐ This poster was created to encourage industrial workers in Canada. Before the United States entered the war in December 1941, Canada was Britain's main supplier of war materiel.

Millions of men were drafted into the armed services and the economy was put on a war footing. By 1943 unemployment had tumbled to 1 per cent, the lowest level ever measured in the United States.

As the demand for weapons and ammunition grew, U.S. companies stopped making consumer goods. Car makers such as General Motors and Ford adapted their factories to make military equipment. The assembly lines that had turned out cars now produced tanks and torpedo bombers. New ways of working

RESOURCES

All combatants relied on natural resources, such as coal, iron or food. Germany and Japan both aimed to increase their supplies from captured territory. Britain relied on imports from the United States and Canada, which had ample supplies of resources.

⇑ **This poster was painted by the U.S. artist Norman Rockwell. It reminds factory workers at home how much the soldiers on the front line depend on them.**

sped up production. The new M-3 machine gun, for example, was made of simple parts stamped out of sheets of metal. It was built by companies that used to make car headlights and jukeboxes.

Digging for Coal

While Britain relied on imports of arms and other goods, it had valuable resources of its own such as coal. Although coal

⇒ **Flying Fortress bombers are assembled at a Boeing aircraft factory in the United States. During the war many companies switched from making consumer goods to military equipment.**

⟹ **'More metal – more arms!' says this poster aimed at encouraging Russian workers. Soviet industry increased its output rapidly. In 1941 factories made 6,590 tanks; the next year, the total was nearly four times as many: 24,446 tanks.**

miners were excused from military service, there were not enough of them to meet demand. So in December 1943 the minister for labour, Ernest Bevin, came up with a new plan. He drafted men to work in the mines in the same way that men were drafted into the services. These 'Bevin's Boys' faced great danger – there were many accidents and deaths – and received low wages. They went on strike in protest. Coal production in Britain actually fell between 1942 and 1945. Many of the Bevin's Boys felt that their contribution to the war effort was often overlooked compared to that of those drafted to the military, even though they had no choice in how they served.

Soviet Industry

In the Soviet Union, agriculture and industry were under the control of the communist government long before war began. Soviet agriculture was based on a policy called collectivisation. The government forced farmers to group together into 'collectives' to try to increase crop production.

Soviet industry was organized by the dictator Joseph Stalin in a series of 'five-year plans'. Each plan set out production targets for factories. The policy seemed to work. By the time Germany invaded in 1941, the Soviet Union was one of the strongest powers in the world in terms of military equipment.

" We need 720,000 men employed in this industry. That is where you boys come in.
ERNEST BEVIN ON BRITISH COAL MINES "

Eyewitness

HOWARD LEE BALL, JNR.

Howard Lee Ball was a young man in a town in New Jersey, United States, which was used to test gunpowder weapons. He recalls the day a new weapon was tested for the first time.

'We were used to all different kinds of explosions. At three-thirty in the afternoon, before, after and during the war, they would test the various things. We'd hear machine guns. You'd hear a machine gun, "Rat-tat-tat-tat-tat". Then, you'd hear, "Ka-boom", and it'd be something else, and then another big boom, and then it would be over. But when this thing went off, and it was about the same time of day that it went off, it ... scared the pants off everybody, and, of course, secrets were secrets. They had the big signs up all around, "Loose Lips Sink Ships", and especially here, in a powder town, and, of course we were afraid of saboteurs, that they would blow the plant up. We were very careful about that.'

ISSUED BY THE MINISTRY OF WAR TRANSPORT AND
THE MINISTRY OF LABOUR AND NATIONAL SERVICE

⇐ **This British poster is a reminder that it wasn't only necessary to recruit war workers: they also had to have places to live and transport to get them to the factory or office.**

There was one problem, however. Most Russian cities, and most factories, were in the west of the country: in the path of the German advance. The answer was simple: move the factories. Soviet workers dismantled 2,500 factories and moved them far to the east. The move saved about 80 per cent of Soviet industry (see box, page 12).

Germany's War Economy

In Germany, Adolf Hitler had counted on a quick war. Industry was not set up for full-scale war production. For the first two years of the war, factories kept making luxury and consumer goods. As the conflict continued, rationing was introduced, first on coal and petrol, then on clothes and food.

In February 1942 Hitler placed Albert Speer in charge of armaments. Fritz Sauckel had the job of mobilizing

LEND–LEASE

In 1940 British prime minister Winston Churchill told U.S. president Franklin D. Roosevelt that Britain was virtually bankrupt. Roosevelt responded by proposing a bill that would allow the United States to sell, lease or lend equipment to any country that the president decided was vital to U.S. security. He compared the war in Europe to a fire in a neighbour's house. If you had a hose, he said, you would lend it to your neighbour and worry about the cost later, if for no other reason than to make sure that your own home did not catch fire next. He told Americans that he wanted the country to become "the arsenal of democracy".

the workforce. Speer and Sauckel had to fill the gaps left by the vast numbers of workers who were now serving on the Eastern Front.

Soon women made up more than 50 per cent of the workforce. The number of foreign workers also rose rapidly: in 1944 it reached 7.8 million. They included not just regular workers in countries that had been occupied by Germany but also prisoners of war and slave labourers. Hundreds of thousands of foreigners were worked to death.

German industry faced many obstacles. The obstacles included a series of Allied bombing raids on key industrial targets. Nevertheless, production remained high until the Allies invaded Germany itself near the end of the war. Working 12 hours a day, seven days a week, German workers were able to increase the production of tanks, artillery and aircraft tenfold between the start of the war and 1944.

⇑ **British boys who are about to start work in coal mines learn about safety underground in a school in Yorkshire in 1940.**

Poor Preparation

Germany's ally, Italy, was among the worst prepared of the major combatants for a modern, 20th-century war. It was the least industrialized of the leading European nations. In addition, it possessed few natural resources.

INVENTIONS

As countries tried to gain a military advantage, the war inspired great technological innovation. The world's first working helicopter was built by the Russian-born U.S. engineer Igor Sikorsky. British scientists developed radar, which used high-frequency radio waves to precisely locate even moving objects. The ultimate research project was the Manhattan Project in which Allied scientists produced the atomic bomb.

⇒ **Unlike an aeroplane, Sikorsky's helicopter did not need a runway and could hover in midair.**

Many of Italy's weapons dated from World War I (1914–1918). A new Italian tank, the Carro Armato, proved a failure. Italy did have a few important industries, such as the giant car maker Fiat, whose factory in Turin was soon turned over to war production. Conditions in the factories were so poor, however, that workers went on strike. They demanded 'bread, peace and freedom'. The demand for war equipment was constantly higher than the supply. Still, it was not until 1943 that the Italian government created a ministry for war production to oversee economic planning for the conflict.

Struggle for Resources

Japan, which with Germany and Italy formed the Axis powers, faced a shortage of natural resources. Its islands lacked agricultural land as well as deposits of oil

ACROSS THE URALS

When the Germans invaded the Soviet Union in 1941, Soviet workers dismantled 2,500 key factories. The equipment was loaded into trucks or onto trains and moved east to the Ural Mountains. There the factories were rebuilt. The workers went, too – up to 25 million people headed east. The evacuation was often chaotic. In addition, the Urals region could not support all the newcomers. Thousands of people died from starvation.

66 *Every blow with the hammer is a blow against the enemy!*

SOVIET POSTER ENCOURAGING INDUSTRY **99**

and metals. It relied on imports for metals and petrol but also for enough rice to feed its population. One of the main reasons Japan went to war was to create the Greater East Asia Co-prosperity Sphere. It would be an empire that would give it access to natural resources.

Industry in Japan was controlled by the *zaibatsu*, or large businesses. The leaders of the *zaibatsu* believed that only military conquest would give them access to overseas sources of raw materials and foreign markets for their goods. The army and big business worked together. Even before the attack on the U.S. fleet at Pearl Harbor in December 1941, industry had switched to military production. The manufacture of luxury goods was banned.

Japan began the war with a series of rapid conquests in Asia. That helped it increase its industrial output, despite losing much of its workforce for military

⇑ **Soviet workers put together tanks at a factory in Chelyabink, east of the Ural Mountains. So many factories were moved to the town that it became known as Tankograd, or 'tank city'.**

⇒ **This U.S. government poster shows an African American working alongside a white colleague. Employers were banned from discriminating against black workers by Executive Order 8802.**

service or agriculture. From a total of 5,088 aircraft in 1941, in 1944 Japanese factories produced more than 28,180.

Although such an increase seems impressive, it hid a looming problem. The production of tanks had fallen by 90 per cent in the same period. Japan was suffering defeats on land as U.S. forces conquered islands across the Pacific, so air power had become far more important to defend Japan itself. U.S. warships and submarines were cutting off Japan's imports by sinking merchant shipping. In 1945 Japan's economy collapsed and industrial output ground to a virtual halt. By then Japan's eventual defeat was virtually inevitable.

BLACK AMERICANS

In 1940 about a quarter of African Americans were unemployed. When the war began, many moved from the South to northern cities to find work. They found factories that insisted on workers from 'north European stock'. In 1941 the black union leader A. Philip Randolph insisted that the defence industry should be open to black workers. He threatened to hold a march on Washington, D.C. Instead, President Roosevelt set up the Fair Employment Practices Commission (FEPC) to protect African American workers from discrimination. By 1944 two million black Americans worked in the defence industries. They still earned less than their white colleagues, however. They often had to live in poor housing. Relations between black and white workers were tense. They sometimes spilled over into violence. In June 1943 race riots in Detroit had to be broken up by 6,000 army troops.

WAR CURRENCY

As Allied armies advanced into enemy territory in North Africa, Europe or Japan, they entered areas where the normal economy had ceased to function. The occupiers printed their own war currency for soldiers and civilians. The bank notes allowed soldiers to buy goods legitimately. They helped to restart local trading.

Paying for the War

Modern warfare is expensive, and World War II was one of the most expensive conflicts in history. How to pay for the war was a problem for politicians on all sides.

The war depended on heavy weapons and technology, so whoever had the strongest economy would be the most probable victor. The nations involved in the fighting had to change their economies to make sure that all economic and industrial activity supported the war effort. The Soviet and Nazi governments already dominated the economies of the Soviet Union and Germany, respectively. They were used to controlling industrial production. But now the democratic governments of Western countries also became more involved in business and industry than ever before. That would have a great impact on life after the war.

⟹ **In this poster from 1941 the Canadian prime minister William Lyon Mackenzie King encourages workers to buy war bonds. The bonds appealed to the buyers' sense of patriotism – they did not pay as much return as other forms of investment.**

⇧ This war currency was issued to U.S. servicemen who were serving in France (top), Germany (centre) and Japan (right) after the fighting had ended.

CONTROLLED INDUSTRY

The German and Soviet governments both had a lot of influence on pre-war industrial production. In Germany, Hitler built up the armed forces despite an international ban. In the Soviet Union, Stalin encouraged rapid industrialization of what had been a mainly agricultural society.

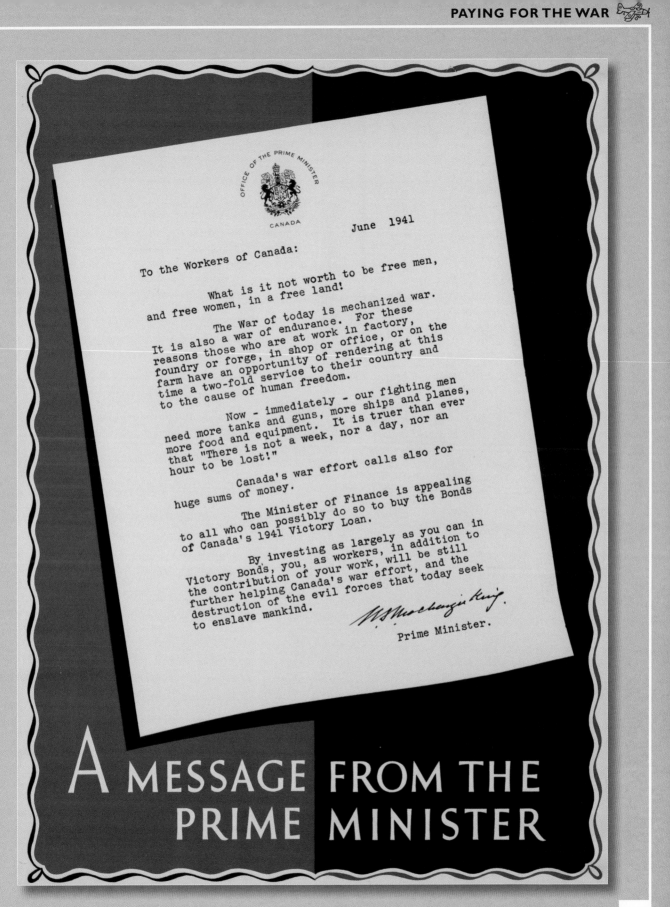

OFFICE OF THE PRIME MINISTER

CANADA

June 1941

To the Workers of Canada:

What is it not worth to be free men, and free women, in a free land!

The War of today is mechanized war. It is also a war of endurance. For these reasons those who are at work in factory, foundry or forge, in shop or office, or on the farm have an opportunity of rendering at this time a two-fold service to their country and to the cause of human freedom.

Now - immediately - our fighting men need more tanks and guns, more ships and planes, more food and equipment. It is truer than ever that "There is not a week, nor a day, nor an hour to be lost!"

Canada's war effort calls also for huge sums of money.

The Minister of Finance is appealing to all who can possibly do so to buy the Bonds of Canada's 1941 Victory Loan.

By investing as largely as you can in Victory Bonds, you, as workers, in addition to the contribution of your work, will be still further helping Canada's war effort, and the destruction of the evil forces that today seek to enslave mankind.

W. S. Mackenzie King

Prime Minister.

A MESSAGE FROM THE PRIME MINISTER

Hidden Costs

Millions of shells, bullets and bombs had to be produced. There were other financial costs, too. Food had to be purchased to feed the civilian and military population. The size of governments grew with the creation of new departments to organize the war effort. Among the millions of people who died in the war were many with unique skills or irreplaceable knowledge. Fighting and bombing destroyed factories, neighbourhoods, even whole cities, and displaced people as refugees. At the end of the war, the countries that had witnessed the worst fighting –

COST OF THE WAR

World War II is estimated to have cost about $1 trillion in 1940s' prices. It is difficult to estimate the actual costs; these are rough figures for the major nations.

United States	$340 billion	Germany	$272 billion
Soviet Union	$192 billion	Japan	$56 billion
Great Britain	$120 billion	Italy	$50 billion
France	$100 billion		

The figures do not include damage caused by the fighting – especially in Britain, China, Germany, Japan, occupied Europe and the Soviet Union – or the human cost of millions of deaths, injuries and displaced refugees.

---

including Germany, China and France – had to spend a huge amount of money on reconstructing businesses and homes.

Raising Money

Governments used different ways to raise the money to pay for the war. In the United States, many people earned good wages, but rationing prevented them from spending too much. The government targeted some of their surplus money by raising income taxes. For every dollar a worker earned, a certain proportion went to the government. Britain, meanwhile, increased its income tax and put a purchase tax on consumer goods.

In both countries, the government effectively borrowed money from its

BUY WAR BONDS

⇐ 'Uncle Sam', a famous symbol of U.S. independence, dominates this poster encouraging Americans to buy war bonds. Because war bonds took money out of circulation, they helped to reduce people's spending and therefore prevent price rises.

American children use their savings to buy war bonds. Everyone was encouraged to buy bonds as part of their patriotic duty.

⇒ Servicemen in uniform are among the crowd attracted by a band performance during a war-bond rally in Times Square in New York City.

citizens in the form of war bonds. These were savings certificates that would pay a certain rate of interest at the end of the war. It became a patriotic gesture to buy bonds. Many schools and community organizations helped boost their sales.

Extensive Campaign

War bonds were promoted in the United States by the biggest advertising campaigns in history. Posters, radio broadcasts and newspaper ads were used to raise public awareness. The artist Norman Rockwell painted four famous posters defining the freedoms the United States was defending. The composer Irving Berlin, who had written 'God Bless America', wrote a theme tune for the campaign called 'Any Bonds Today?'

" Without American production, the Allies could never have won the war.

JOSEPH STALIN, 1943

Eyewitness

GEORGE C. MARSHALL

U.S. general George C. Marshall assessed the state of Europe's economies at the end of the war.

'Machinery has fallen into disrepair or is entirely obsolete. Under Nazi rule, virtually every possible enterprise was geared into the German war machine.... In many countries, confidence in the local currency has been severely shaken. The breakdown of the business structure of Europe during the war was complete.'

The campaign was backed with bond rallies. These public meetings featured celebrities – usually Hollywood stars – making public appearances to urge people to buy bonds. In 'Stars Over America', more than 330 stars toured more than 300 towns and cities. Sports teams held special matches at which a war bond was used instead of a ticket for admission. By the end of the

⇒ **Red Cross members in Britain raise money to help alleviate hunger in the Soviet Union. The Russians relied on foreign aid because Germany's invasion devastated their own economy.**

war, more than 85 million Americans – over half of the population – had bought bonds worth $185.7 billion.

U.S. Loans

The United States was the world's richest power. It gave credit to its allies, mainly Britain and the Soviet Union, in the form of lend–lease (see box, page 10). This scheme allowed the Allies to buy U.S. military materiel but to delay paying for it until after the war. Both Britain and Russia ran up huge debts: Britain did not make its final repayment until 2006.

U.S. credit was also important in the aftermath of the war. A huge amount of damage had been caused. In Poland, for

⇐ **This Japanese poster declares 'Buy war bonds' – but Japanese war production faced a huge challenge. At the start of the war, for example, most of the army's trucks were U.S. imports. Once the war began, spare parts were no longer available.**

> *We'll all be blessed*
> *If we invest*
> *In the U.S.A.*
>
> 'ANY BONDS TODAY?', IRVING BERLIN

example, 30 per cent of buildings were damaged. Germany had been devastated by the combined Allied advance from east and west. It seemed to some observers that allowing Germany to remain bankrupt would cause economic instability in Europe. This would slow down the recovery of the world economy after the war. The United States therefore loaned Germany and other European countries $13 billion to get their manufacturing running again. A similar process took place in Japan, where the economy recovered rapidly after the war.

⟹ **United China Relief was formed in 1941 to bring together U.S. charities working in China. Although the main purpose of the organization was to care for the sick or for refugees, it also funded guerrilla units fighting the Japanese inside China.**

OPERATION BERNHARD

In 1943 a bank in Tangiers, in Morocco, discovered a fake British bank note that was an almost perfect forgery. It was part of Operation Bernhard, a German plan to flood Britain with forged money. A printing press was set up with a team of expert forgers recruited from the Sachsenhausen concentration camp to produce nearly 9 million forged notes to be dropped by aircraft. The Germans hoped that the British would spend the money, causing prices to rise rapidly, so destroying the economy. No-one knows if the plan would have worked. It was eventually cancelled because of a lack of available aircraft to drop the money.

Shortages and Rationing

With the war effort taking priority, and using the great majority of essential resources, there were not enough food or other goods to go around.

All vital materials were required for war industries, which left civilians with only limited supplies of goods such as oil, steel, rubber and food.

Rationing and Recycling

One common response to shortages was rationing. Families were provided with a weekly or yearly allocation of coupons, based on their number of members, for scarce items such as petrol or shoes (leather and rubber were in short supply). Governments also ran campaigns to recycle materials. In Britain, iron fence railings were taken down from public parks, homes and even the gardens of Buckingham Palace to be melted down.

WASTE THE FOOD
AND
HELP THE HUN

⇑ This British poster reminded people that wasting any food would help Adolf Hitler and the 'Hun', a disrespectful slang term for the Germans. Another poster read: 'Food wasted is another ship lost'.

⇒ Posters featuring the Squander Bug were displayed at British railway stations and in town centres to discourage shoppers from making unnecessary purchases.

WHAT WAS IN SHORT SUPPLY?

Everyone knows that foods were rationed during the war, along with metals and petrol. But some other shortages may not be so obvious. Because paper was in short supply, people largely gave up sending Christmas cards. When typewriter factories switched to war production, there was soon a shortage of typewriters, which at the time were essential for all kinds of government and office work. Birdwatchers gave up their binoculars for ships' lookouts. People surrendered their dogs to the military canine corps. There were fewer and fewer rubber bands to hold things together: eventually they were completely replaced by sticky tape. On both sides of the Atlantic there was no nylon or silk to make women's stockings. Many women used colouring to paint their legs and then used an eye pencil to draw a line down the back, like the seam on real stockings.

In the United States, boy scouts helped collect unwanted pots and old tin cans on scrap drives. The Japanese government forced its citizens to hand over even safety pins and metal spectacle frames. Hundreds of thousands of worn-out car and lorry tyres were collected and recycled into new tyres for military use.

Reducing Consumption

Clothes were rationed because material was required to make military uniforms, parachutes or other war equipment. In Britain a campaign urged women to 'Make do and mend' – to repair old clothes and household items rather than buy new ones. In the United States a campaign urged people to 'Use it up, wear it out, make it do, or do without.'

When it came to new clothes, the main concern was utility, or usefulness. Too many pockets or button holes were forbidden because they used more material. The same standard applied to other consumer goods, such as furniture. Utility furniture was plain, with few decorations. It could only usually be bought by people who had just got married or families whose homes had been bombed.

⇑ **American Boy Scouts tip out metal they have collected on a scrap drive. The metal was melted down and used to produce aircraft, warships, tanks and ammunition … anything that could help the war effort.**

ONE PENNY

Stands Supreme   NO. 13,628   ∗ ∗ ∗   FRIDAY, DECEMBER 29, 1939

RATIONING TO WIN WAR
Saving Currency and Cargo Room   TROOPS SEARCH

SUGAR (12 OZ.) JAN. 8: MEAT LATER ON

By Daily Mail Reporter

RATIONING of sugar—at 12 oz. weekly from January 8—and meat—in February—announced yesterday by the Food Minister, Mr. W. S. Morrison, will be every housewife's New Year contribution

⇐ **Britain's *Daily Mail* newspaper announces new restrictions on rations on 29 December 1939. The article went on to assure Britons that the port at New York was crammed with supplies ready to be shipped to the Allies.**

DON'T WASTE WATER

PHILADELPHIA COUNCIL OF DEFENSE

PENNA ART WPA

⬅ It was important to make the most of everything, including water. Americans were encouraged to fix leaky taps, turn off the water while shaving or brushing their teeth and to use dirty bath water in the garden.

No. 108676 EH
UNITED STATES OF AMERICA
OFFICE OF PRICE ADMINISTRATION

4

WAR RATION BOOK FOUR

Issued to *Rosalind J. Sandler*
(Print first, middle, and last names)

Complete address *218 Forest St.*

Marshall, Michigan

READ BEFORE SIGNING
In accepting this book, I recognize that it remains the property of the United States Government. I will use it only in the manner and for the purposes authorized by the Office of Price Administration.

Void if Altered _____
(Signature)

It is a criminal offense to violate rationing regulations.

OPA Form R-145

AFC. 2001/001/2671

⬆ All American families were issued with ration books based on the number of family members and their needs. Everyone was entitled to the same allowances.

Food Supplies

The war interrupted food supplies in all combatant countries. In Britain, which relied on imported food, German submarines prevented food getting through. There was a danger that Britain would be starved into surrender. The government rationed food in order to share it out equally. Each family was issued coupons for certain types of food, which they exchanged with shopkeepers. Meanwhile, government campaigns urged people to 'Dig for Victory'.

THE BLACK MARKET

Rationing encouraged an illegal trade, or 'black market', in restricted goods. Often it was no more serious than persuading farmers to provide, say, an extra egg or two. But many consumers had cash to pay higher prices to get around ration limits. In Britain, goods sent from the United States for U.S. bases often found their way onto the black market, particularly clothing and alcohol. In the United States, there was an illicit trade in meat, sugar and petrol. Many people resented the black market. It undermined the feeling that everyone was pulling together and enduring the same shortages.

⇐ **A starving Russian couple search for food in a pile of potato peelings left outside a factory destroyed by the retreating German armies.**

Many people started vegetable gardens. Even traffic islands were dug up and used to grow fruit and vegetables or to raise a few chickens or pigs for extra eggs and meat. In the United States, the Office of Price Administration rationed scarce goods, starting with sugar but later including meat, butter and tinned food.

Here, too, the government ran a campaign to encourage people to grow food in 'Victory Gardens'.

New recipes made the most of the limited food available. In one campaign the cartoon characters Doctor Carrot and Potato Pete encouraged the British to make the most of vegetables. Walt Disney

LAND GIRLS

About 30,000 British farm workers joined the military. Their place was taken by members of the Women's Land Army (WLA), which was introduced in 1939. By 1944 about 80,000 Land Girls had volunteered or had been conscripted to serve on the land. Most came from rural communities themselves.

⇒ **Land Girls come to grips with a pair of large turkeys. The WLA was based on a similar organization used in World War I; from 1943 a similar scheme was used in the United States.**

> **"** *Use it up, wear it out, make it do,*
> *or do without.*
> **AMERICAN ADVERTISING CAMPAIGN** **"**

⇓ **Storing food was just as important as growing it. People were encouraged to use fruit and vegetables to make jams, chutneys and pickles to use in the winter.**

provided cartoons of carrots to help the popularity campaign. The British government promoted Woolton Pie, named after the minister for food. It was made from parsnips, carrots and potato, with flavour added by herbs.

Facing Starvation

If shortages were bad in Britain and the United States, in the Soviet Union, Germany and Japan they were at times even worse. In the Soviet city of Leningrad, which was besieged by the Germans for 900 days, supplies could only be brought in by truck across a frozen lake. Civilians were allowed only 225 g (8 oz) of bread per day. They ate dogs and cats in desperation. Still people died in the streets (the city had no electricity and no fuel for heating or transportation).

The Axis Countries

In Germany, rationing was introduced early in the war. The allowances fell dramatically as Germany's enemies advanced. In 1939 adults could have unlimited bread; by late October 1942 that had fallen to 2.125 kg (4.5 lb) a month; by April 1945, it was only 900 g (2 lb). The amounts of meat and fats had also been cut to about a quarter of what they had been in 1939.

Even in peacetime, Japan was never able to produce enough food to feed all

"We'll have lots to eat this winter, won't we Mother?"

Grow your own
Can your own

its civilians. It had to import 22 per cent of its rice, which was the staple food in the Japanese diet. More than 80 per cent of sugar had to be imported. Despite government controls and rationing there was barely enough to go around.

By late 1944 most people could find a little fish but no meat, although some people ate cats and dogs. Most people received only 225 g (8 oz) of rice a day, and a few vegetables. By the end of the war, many people no longer received any rice rations. Starvation was common.

A British family poses with its official rations for a year. It was often possible to add to the basic allowance with other foods that were not rationed.

Weekly ration for an adult, Britain, 1942

113 g (4 oz) lard or butter
340 g (12 oz) sugar
113 g (4 oz) bacon
2 eggs
170 g (6 oz) meat
57 g (2 oz) tea
(Bread, potatoes, vegetables and fish were not rationed but were not always available)

Weekly ration for an American citizen, 1943

0.9 kg (2 lb) canned food
340 g (12 oz) sugar
114 g (4 oz) cheese
1.1 kg (2.5 lb) meat
The coffee allowance was 0.4 kg (1 lb) every 5 weeks

STARVATION

In areas devastated by war or under enemy occupation, food sometimes disappeared altogether. In Holland, for example, 18,000 people died in a famine in 1944; in occupied Athens, Greece, more than 300,000 civilians starved to death.

Overall Effects

Overall the arrival of rationing had a positive effect. In particular, poor people ate more healthily than before. The system made sure that everyone had equal supplies of nutritious food, no matter what their income was. In Britain, for example, everyone received daily milk, orange juice and cod-liver oil for essential nutrients and vitamins. The number of children having school meals doubled from 1940 to 1941.

The ration system also helped to create a feeling that everyone was suffering together. While workers had good jobs and earned more money than before the war, wealthier people found themselves worse off. New taxes hit luxury goods, so people bought less. Everyone's clothes began to look more similar. Few people could drive their cars or take luxury holidays. That all helped make society seem a little fairer, which made people more content with their lot.

CARROT HOT POT

This recipe was devised to encourage the use of carrots, accompanied by a Walt Disney cartoon of 'Carroty George'. Carrot also featured in the so-called 'Austerity Pudding', made with potato, grated carrot and apple, dried fruit, dried egg, flour, breadcrumbs, cooking fat and a tiny amount of golden syrup or marmalade.

You can meet young Carroty George any day at the 'Hot Pot'.... He's a fellow of tact and resource and can so quickly adapt himself to any occasion, sweet or savoury. See how well he fits into Carrot Hot Pot:

I. Coarsely grate 6 carrots and 6 potatoes; mix with 2 tablespoons packet sage and onion. Make seasoning of 2 teaspoons salt, ½ teaspoon pepper, and, if possible, brown sugar. Put half the vegetables in a stew pot, cover with half the seasoning, add rest of vegetables and rest of seasoning.

2. No water required, cover stew pot and bake very slowly for 2 hours. You'll have a dish very much out of the ordinary, for three or four.

⇒ This ration card belonged to a citizen in Berlin. Sections were filled in as allowances were bought. As the Russians advanced on the German capital from the east and the other Allies aproached from the west, food supplies became very short for most people.

Women at War

Before World War II, women in virtually all countries worked mainly in the home. That changed when the absence of men caused a labour shortage in industry and business.

The war improved opportunities for many women, particularly in employment. In most countries almost all men of working age were either in the military or employed in essential jobs. Employers had to find other workers – mainly among women.

Changes in Women's Work

Women already worked before the war, of course. Many played a huge role on family farms, while jobs such as nursing and teaching were traditionally done by women. But in 1939 most women were still excluded from jobs in factories or modern parts of the economy. The shortage of workers during the war, however, meant that women took on many traditionally male jobs.

⟹ 'We will take their places' declares this Soviet poster of 1941. Within two years, women made up over half of the industrial workforce.

```
WOMEN AT WORK
Before the war
it was unusual
for women to work
outside the home.
Working women were
often single or
had no children;
they gave up their
jobs when they got
married or when
they had a baby.
Traditional women's
jobs included
nursing, teaching
and working in
offices as typists.
```

WOMEN IN COMBAT

Few countries allowed women to serve at the front: an exception was the Soviet Union. About 800,000 Soviet women were drafted as snipers, tank drivers or pilots. The 46th Guards Night Bomber Aviation Regiment were known as the 'Night Witches'. The famous fighter pilot Lily Litvak was nicknamed the 'White Rose of Stalingrad' for her heroism in defending the city.

⟹ Russian infantry women march through a village on their way to the front.

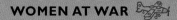

ROSIE THE RIVETER

Rosie the Riveter, first mentioned in a song in 1942, became an icon for American women. She was a patriotic assembly line worker, supporting the war effort. The War Manpower Commission used her as a model for their movie and poster campaigns aimed at persuading women to take traditionally male jobs. There were many Rosies, although some people associate the character with Rose Will Monroe, a woman who welded bombers at a plant in Michigan. The most famous portrayal of Rosie was in a 1942 poster painted by J. Howard Miller entitled We Can Do It!

⇐ J. Howard Miller's famous poster of Rosie was also turned into postage stamps. Miller's original image was only displayed for a few weeks, after which it was replaced by the next in his series of patriotic posters.

In the United States, some 30,000 women took dangerous – but highly paid – work in munitions factories. Other women worked on assembly lines, where they built ships and aircraft. A famous poster campaign highlighted Rosie the Riveter, who became a symbol of women's strength and resolve (see box).

In Britain, a law of December 1941 made women between the ages of 18 and 50 available for national service. Many took on 'male' jobs, including welding, farming, or driving buses. It was virtually impossible for a woman to avoid work unless she had a family to look after or she had war workers staying in her home.

The Nazi View

In Germany, the Nazi Party promoted a traditional view of women. The ideal German woman was a mother and homemaker. They belonged in the home, not in the workplace. Adolf Hitler himself actually argued against using women workers in industry.

Over the first two years of the war, the number of German women who had jobs actually fell. By 1942, however, the government realized that they had to involve women in the war effort, despite Hitler's opposition. By 1944 about 10.5 million men had been called into the military services and women made up

French nurses look after a wounded soldier near the front line in France in 1944. Volunteering for the medical services was a popular way for many women to become directly involved in the war effort.

⇊ Russian women make munitions in a factory in Moscow. Such work could be dangerous, because it involved the use of gunpowder.

> 66 *If you've used an electric mixer in the kitchen, you can learn to run a drill press.*
> AMERICAN WAR MANPOWER CAMPAIGN 99

about 50 per cent of the industrial workforce. That was still a lower percentage than in Britain, the United States or the Soviet Union, where women filled 55 per cent of all jobs.

Women and the Military

Many women were involved in the military effort. A few actually fought, mainly in the Soviet Union. More often, women served as nurses or drivers or did other support tasks. The U.S. Women's Auxiliary Ferrying Squadron delivered aircraft from factories to air bases. Women also served as test pilots in the United States and Germany.

GERMAN WOMEN AT WORK

The Nazi party in Germany saw a woman's role as that of being a good wife and mother. Despite the efforts of Hermann Goring and Albert Speer to get more women into munitions factories, Hitler remained opposed to the move for the first years of the war. In 1943, the government finally conscripted all women between the ages of 17 and 45 but the measure was unpopular and many exemptions were allowed. Germany filled its employment gap with captured foreign workers, who included many women. Nevertheless, German women did work in factories and in agriculture. At the end of the war, they helped to rebuild towns and cities, often using basic tools and their bare hands.

⇐ **A woman in Berlin cooks for her hungry family at the end of the war. The responsibility for finding food in times of great shortage often fell to women, who were left to look after their children.**

Half a million British women joined the Women's Royal Navy Service, the Auxiliary Territorial Service and the Women's Auxiliary Air Force. More than 80,000 served in the Women's Land Army, which worked in agriculture; more than 400,000 also worked in civil defence, as air-raid wardens or as members of the Home Guard.

A Positive View

For many women, the war years ultimately brought a welcome change in their traditional role. Not only did the demand for work take them out of the house, it also often brought them into contact with new friends in the workplace. The income they earned also

⇐ **A mother and baby feature on this Nazi poster with a quote from Adolf Hitler: 'The individual must and will die, but the people must endure.'**

Der Einzelne muss und wird wie immer vergehn, allein

DAS VOLK MUSS BLEIBEN

CARING FOR THE FAMILY

For many women, the war brought new challenges: not just in having to go to work, but also in being the sole carer for their families. With so many men serving away from home, this was true everywhere. Women became the head of the household, as well as being responsible for looking after their children's upbringing. Grandparents and older children often helped by taking on extra responsibility for the family. As defeat threatened Germany and Japan, women there had the additional challenge of overcoming sometimes severe shortages of food to feed their families.

made them more independent than before, when they often had to rely on their husbands for money.

At the end of the war, when jobs were often reclaimed by returning servicemen, some women found it difficult to accept the limitations of a traditional life looking after the home and family. Often they took other jobs to try to remain in the labour market. That led to upheaval for some families. The changes in the traditional roles of father and mother placed great strain on some marriages. Some of the men returning from the war found it difficult to accept the new position of women at work.

A Long-Lasting Effect

The war had a long-lasting impact on how women were viewed by society. Some people had predicted that it would take two or three women to perform a job previously done by a man. In fact, women performed just as well as men. In 1945 the British government acknowledged that when it set up a commission on equal pay for men and women. Achieving equal pay, however, would take many more years.

THE WAR AND FASHION

The war did not entirely prevent women from dressing well. Some liked to keep up appearances by, for example, wearing lipstick or having long hair like the movie star Veronica Lake. But shortages of textiles limited the clothes available. In Britain, the Civilian Clothing Order of 1941 banned excess decoration, including buttons, trimmings, pleats or pockets. London fashion designers responded by coming up with 34 'utility' designs that followed the new rules. For many women, however, such clothes were an unimaginable luxury. They knitted their own or followed official advice to 'make do and mend'.

⇐ 'Soldier, answer the Motherland with victory!' declares this Russian poster. The woman echoes a traditional female symbol of the country, Mother Russia.

ВОИН, ОТВЕТЬ РОДИНЕ ПОБЕДОЙ !

Children and Evacuation

The war had a huge impact on children in the nations involved in the conflict. In places like Ukraine, France, Italy and Germany, daily life was virtually put on hold.

Schools or homes were damaged or destroyed. Whole families had become refugees, uprooted from their everyday life. They were more concerned about finding food and shelter than about education or children's games.

Avoiding Enemy Bombing

In Britain and other countries, schoolchildren learned gas-mask drills so they could protect themselves in case of gas attack. When the German night-time bombing campaign known as the Blitz began against British cities in September 1940, whole families slept in bomb shelters or in the tunnels of the London Underground. Later in the war, German and Japanese children and their families were caught up in massive Allied bombing raids on cities such as Dresden and Tokyo. In Britain and other countries, many children were sent out of the cities to live far from home with strangers in rural areas (see box Evacuation, left). The countryside was thought to be far safer, because enemy bombers were usually aiming for factories and other urban targets.

⬇ **The *Star* reports the successful evacuation of London's children on 1 September 1939. In fact, there were many problems and many evacuees had upsetting experiences.**

London's Children Were Grand

EVACUATION of thousands of London children was carried out to-day without a hitch.

There were smiles everywhere, and hardly a tear.

And soon from the reception areas came reports of the warm and friendly welcomes that were given to the little ones on their arrival.

The evacuation was a triumph of good organisation.

A visitor to London would hardly have realised that it was happening at all. Not one big traffic hold-up was reported, and people had remarkably little difficulty in catching trains and buses.

CITY AND COUNTRY

Evacuation brought two parts of Britain in contact for the first time. Some rural people feared that city children would be dirty or dishonest. Meanwhile, some children from the cities had never seen cows or other animals. They were also not used to helping with farm work – or with eating so much fresh food.

The spirit of Hitler urges a mother to take her children to the city in this British poster. Some evacuees were away from their families for up to five years.

The British evacuation plan, named Operation Pied Piper, began at the start of the war. It had planned for the evacuation of some 3.5 million children from six industrial cities, including the capital, London. In the end, some 1.9 million children were evacuated in August 1939. Although some had their mothers with them, most were on their own. Many had moved back to their homes by the end of the year, when the expected German air attacks did not actually occur.

⇑ **A British teacher supervises students in a gas-mask drill in September 1939. Although the fear of gas attack was so high in Britain at the start of the war that everyone had to carry their gas masks at all times, no such attacks actually occurred.**

The war affected children's lives in a variety of ways. The shortages that other people suffered also applied to children. Some foods were unavailable or in short supply (there were still children in Britain in the 1950s who had never seen a banana). Sweets and treats like biscuits were rare. Comics were rarer, because paper was limited, although it was still possible to get hold of books (as long as they were not illustrated). Many beaches were closed, so holidays at the seaside became a thing of the past. In Britain, however, some children found an exciting new place to play: bomb sites.

Lavoratori d'Italia!
I "Liberatori" già da oggi pensano per l'avvenire dei vostri figli...

⇐ **Children often featured in propaganda like this Italian poster showing a British soldier dragging away two terrified children. The poster urges: 'Italian workers! The "liberators" are already thinking about the future of your children.'**

Eyewitness

JOYCE BIDMEAD

In 1940 Joyce Bidmead was evacuated with her sisters from London in 1940 to Weston-Super-Mare in the west of England.

'Miss Standish had wrinkles that reminded me of the walnuts we ate at Christmas. She was an elderly spinster who lived in Swiss Road. She was kind, but not used to looking after children. I remember having burnt fried bread and dripping for breakfast and spam and lumpy mashed potato for tea. My two sisters were homesick and cried every night. I cried too, but hid under the bedclothes so they would not hear me. We wrote home regularly, telling mum and dad how happy we were. In fact we were miserable.'

⇓ A report in the *Daily Express* of 26 July 1943 reports that 16-year-old Germans are fighting the Allies in Sicily. Although the boys were only school age, they were part of the elite Hermann Göring Division.

The blackout meant that few people went out in the evening. Children and their families played board and card games such as Beetle Drive or Housey Housey. The radio was also a popular way to pass the time.

Going to School

For many children, school continued much as normal. Children still had to take exams, for example. There were some significant changes, however. During evacuation in Britain, for example, many schools were opened in pubs or church halls. Teachers were excluded from the draft, but so many male teachers had volunteered to go to war that classrooms were dominated by women teachers. That was also true in the United States and virtually all other fighting countries.

After school it was difficult for students to do homework if there was an air raid. The danger of raids also meant that families had to sleep in shelters in their gardens or in communal locations.

That often meant that people did not sleep well – making it more difficult for children to concentrate at school the next day.

In the classroom, meanwhile, there were changes to the regular timetable. Students learned about air-raid drills and followed the progress of the war. They were also encouraged to join in patriotic activities to support the war effort. That might take the form of raising money to pay for military goods or of classroom

HITLER YOUTH

The Hitler Youth was set up in 1933 to educate German boys in Nazi philosophy; in 1936 it was taken over by the state and made compulsory. From age 10, boys with "pure" Aryan blood joined the German Young People before joining the Hitler Youth at age 13. The boy was trained in self-discipline and Nazi views. At age 18, the young man joined the party and entered the armed forces or the state labour service.

actitivies such as knitting clothes that could be sent to the troops. Children were encouraged to save up to buy war bonds. Organizations such as the Boy Scouts and Girl Guides meant that children could spend some of their leisure time helping the war effort, too.

Militaristic Societies

In Germany and Japan, the incorporation of children into the war effort went further than in the Allied countries. Adolf Hitler and the Japanese military government both believed that youth should be organized to become part of the military effort. In Germany, youth organizations made sure that boys and girls were brought up to believe in the values of the Nazi Party. The Hitler Youth was set up on military lines, with uniforms, weapons training and strict discipline. The female equivalent – the

⇐ **'Youth serves the Führer', urges this German poster, 'All 10-year-olds into the Hitler Youth'. In 1936, when membership became compulsory, the Hitler Youth had some 5.4 million members.**

> **A young German must be swift as a greyhound, as tough as leather, and as hard as Krupp's steel.**
>
> ADOLF HITLER

In Germany, for example, young people were educated by the various youth groups to see the Nazi Party as their real 'family'. They were encouraged to report their parents if they showed signs of not supporting the war effort.

Elsewhere, many men were away from home on military service. They could be absent for years. Children were left to be brought up by their mothers. Many women also had to go out to work for the first time in factories or other related war work, and left their children in the care of grandparents or neighbours. Older siblings in particular often had to take responsibility for their brothers and sisters. But in reality all children had to grow up quickly in order to adapt to the unusual conditions of wartime.

⇐ **British boys play at being soldiers. In a militarized society in which many men were in uniform, it was perhaps no surprise that even children's games echoed the conflict that was being fought in Europe and the Pacific.**

League of German Girls – prepared young women for motherhood and running the home. Eventually, the members of the Hitler Youth would be called upon to fight in the Battle for Berlin in 1945. In Japan, meanwhile, schools produced students who were physically fit and trained in military drill. Again, teenagers ended up taking part in actual fighting in large numbers towards the end of the conflict.

Family Life

In all countries, one of the most obvious ways in which the war affected children was in the changes it brought to families.

Eyewitness

EVELYN WHITAKER

German-American Evelyn Whitaker describes the childhood memories of her mother, who grew up in Germany during World War II.

'Their food consisted of mostly cabbage and bread. Sometimes my grandmother would stand in line for a whole day for just one loaf of bread only to find out they were all gone when it was her turn to get some. During this time, many families would take their children out of school at a young age – 12 years old for many – so that they could go to work and help the family survive. My grandmother despite the temptation would not allow this. Having her children get an education was too important to her, so as her children slept she sewed and sewed to make what little money she could. For the children that did leave school to work, the most popular places to work at were bakeries and any place that made food. This way at least you could bring some leftover food home to your family at the end of the day.'

Timeline of World War II

1939

SEPTEMBER:
German troops invade and overrun Poland
Britain and France declare war on Germany
The Soviet Union invades eastern Poland and extends control to the Baltic states
The Battle of the Atlantic begins
NOVEMBER:
The Soviet Union launches a winter offensive against Finland

1940

APRIL:
Germany invades Denmark and Norway
Allied troops land in Norway
MAY:
Germany invades Luxembourg, the Netherlands, Belgium and France
Allied troops are evacuated at Dunkirk
JUNE:
Italy declares war on France and Britain
German troops enter Paris
France signs an armistice with Germany
Italy bombs Malta in the Mediterranean
JULY:
German U-boats inflict heavy losses on Allied convoys in the Atlantic
Britain sends warships to neutralise the French fleet in North Africa
The Battle of Britain begins
SEPTEMBER:
Luftwaffe air raids begin the Blitz – the bombing of London and other British cities
Italian troops advance from Libya into Egypt
Germany, Italy and Japan sign the Tripartite Pact
OCTOBER:
Italy invades Greece; Greek forces, aided by the British, mount a counterattack
DECEMBER:
British troops at Sidi Barrani, Egypt, force the Italians to retreat

1941

JANUARY:
Allied units capture Tobruk in Libya
British forces in Sudan attack Italian East Africa
FEBRUARY:
Allies defeat Italy at Benghazi, Libya
Rommel's Afrika Korps arrive in Tripoli
MARCH:
The Africa Korps drive British troops back from El Agheila
APRIL:
German, Italian and Hungarian units invade Yugoslavia
German forces invade Greece
The Afrika Korps beseige Tobruk
MAY:
The British sink the German battleship *Bismarck*
JUNE:
German troops invade the Soviet Union
JULY:
German forces advance to within 16 kilometres (10 miles) of Kiev
AUGUST:
The United States bans the export of oil to Japan
SEPTEMBER:
German forces start the siege of Leningrad
German Army Group Centre advances on Moscow
NOVEMBER:
British troops begin an attack to relieve Tobruk
The Allies liberate Ethiopia
DECEMBER:
Japanese aircraft attack the U.S. Pacific Fleet at Pearl Harbor
Japan declares war on the United States and Britain
The United States, Britain and the Free French declare war on Japan
Japanese forces invade the Philippines, Malaya and Thailand, and defeat the British garrison in Hong Kong

1942

JANUARY:
Japan attacks the Dutch East Indies and invades Burma
Rommel launches a new offensive in Libya

FEBRUARY:
Singapore surrenders to the Japanese
APRIL:
The Bataan Peninsula in the Philippines falls to the Japanese
MAY:
U.S. and Japanese fleets clash at the Battle of the Coral Sea
Rommel attacks the Gazala Line in Libya
JUNE:
The U.S. Navy defeats the Japanese at the Battle of Midway
Rommel recaptures Tobruk and the Allies retreat to Egypt
JULY:
The Germans take Sebastopol after a long siege and advance
    into the Caucasus
AUGUST:
U.S. Marines encounter fierce Japanese resistance in the
    Solomons
SEPTEMBER–OCTOBER:
Allied forces defeat Axis troops at El Alamein, Egypt – the first
    major Allied victory of the war
NOVEMBER:
U.S. and British troops land in Morocco and Algeria

1943

FEBRUARY:
The German Sixth Army surrenders at Stalingrad
The Japanese evacuate troops from Guadalcanal in the Solomons
MAY:
Axis forces in Tunisia surrender, ending the campaign in North
    Africa
JULY:
U.S. troops make landings on New Georgia Island in the
    Solomons
The Red Army wins the Battle of Kursk
Allied troops land on Sicily
British bombers conduct massive raids on Hamburg
AUGUST:
German forces occupy Italy
SEPTEMBER:
Allied units begin landings on mainland Italy
Italy surrenders, prompting a German invasion of northern
    Italy
OCTOBER:
The Red Army liberates the Caucasus
NOVEMBER:
U.S. carrier aircraft attack Rabaul in the Solomons

1944

JANUARY:
The German siege of Leningrad ends
FEBRUARY:
U.S. forces conquer the Marshall Islands

MARCH:
The Soviet offensive reaches the Dniester River
Allied aircraft bomb the monastery at Monte Cassino
    in Italy
JUNE:
U.S. troops enter the city of Rome
D-Day–the Allies begin the invasion of northern Europe
U.S. aircraft defeat the Japanese fleet at the Battle of the
    Philippine Sea
JULY:
The Red Army begins its offensive to clear the Baltic states
Soviet tanks enter Poland
AUGUST:
Japanese troops withdraw from Myitkyina in Burma
French forces liberate Paris
Allied units liberate towns in France, Belgium and the
    Netherlands
OCTOBER:
Soviet and Yugoslavian troops capture Belgrade, the
    Yugoslav capital
The Japanese suffer defeat at the Battle of Leyte Gulf
DECEMBER:
Hitler counterattacks in the Ardennes in the Battle of
    the Bulge

1945

JANUARY:
The U.S. Army lands on Luzon in the Philippines
The Red Army liberates Auschwitz
Most of Poland and Czechoslovakia are liberated by
    the Allies
FEBRUARY:
U.S. troops take the Philippine capital, Manila
U.S. Marines land on the island of Iwo Jima
Soviet troops strike west across Germany
The U.S. Army heads towards the River Rhine
APRIL:
U.S. troops land on the island of Okinawa
Mussolini is shot by partisans
Soviet troops assault Berlin
Hitler commits suicide in his bunker
MAY:
All active German forces surrender
JUNE:
Japanese resistance ends in Burma and on Okinawa
AUGUST:
Atomic bombs are dropped on Hiroshima and Nagasaki
Japan surrenders

World War II: Europe

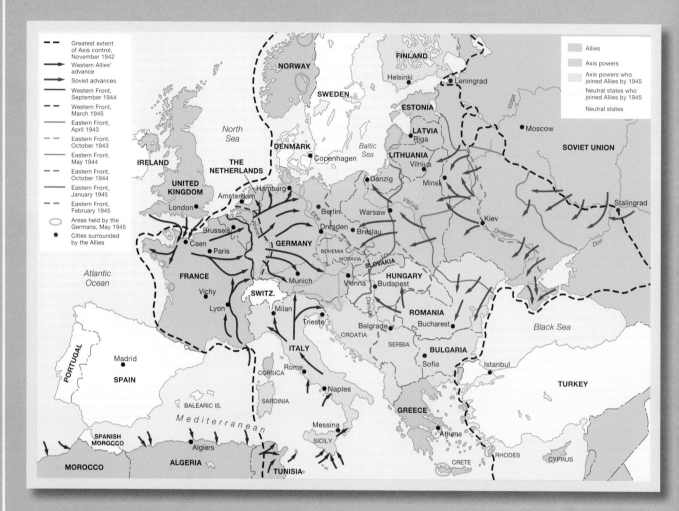

The legend and map labels include:

- Greatest extent of Axis control, November 1942
- Western Allies' advance
- Soviet advances
- Western Front, September 1944
- Western Front, March 1945
- Eastern Front, April 1943
- Eastern Front, October 1943
- Eastern Front, May 1944
- Eastern Front, October 1944
- Eastern Front, January 1945
- Eastern Front, February 1945
- Areas held by the Germans, May 1945
- Cities surrounded by the Allies

- Allies
- Axis powers
- Axis powers who joined Allies by 1945
- Neutral states who joined Allies by 1945
- Neutral states

The war began with rapid German advances through the Low Countries and northern France. In June 1941 German armies struck through eastern Europe into the Soviet Union, besieging Leningrad and Stalingrad. However, Allied landings in North Africa led to eventual victory there and opened the way for the invasion of Sicily and then of the Italian peninsula itself, forcing Italy to surrender. In the east the defeat of the German Sixth Army at Stalingrad forced a long retreat during which German forces were harried by communist guerrillas at all moments. In June 1944 Allied forces landed in northern France on D-Day and began to fight their way towards Berlin. As the Soviet advance closed in and the Americans and British crossed the Rhine River into Germany, defeat became inevitable. Hitler committed suicide in his bunker at the heart of his failed Reich, or empire.

World War II: The Pacific

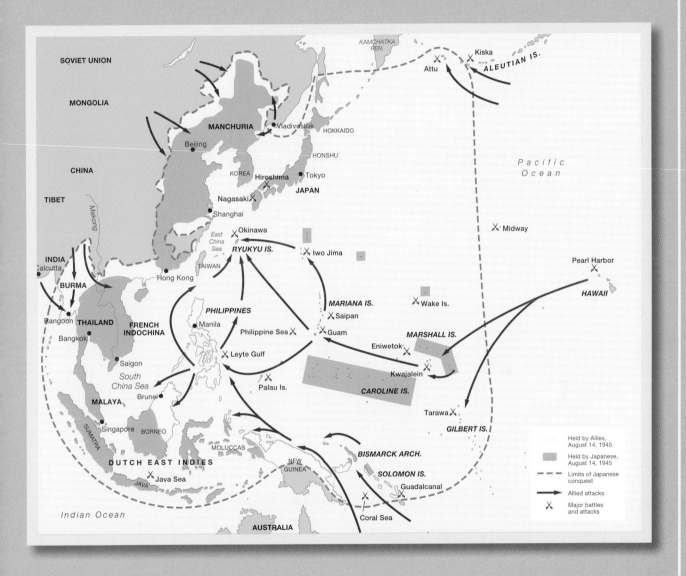

The Pacific conflict began with swift Japanese advances and occupation of territory throughout Southeast Asia, Malaya, the East Indies, the Philippines and the island groups of the Pacific. The U.S. fleet was weakened by the attack on Pearl Harbor, but the damage it suffered was repaired remarkably quickly. After the naval victory at Midway in June 1942, U.S. commanders fought a campaign of 'island hopping', overcoming strong local Japanese resistance to establish a series of stepping stones that would bring their bombers close enough to attack the Japanese home islands. Meanwhile, British and Indian troops pushed back the Japanese advance from Burma.

Biographies

Neville Chamberlain

British statesman. Conservative prime minister from 1937 to 1940, Chamberlain led the policy of appeasement of Hitler. He argued that giving in to Hitler's demands was the best way to prevent war. When the policy failed, he resigned in favour of Winston Churchill.

Churchill, Winston

British statesman. Churchill became British prime minister in May 1940 after a controversial political career. He was an energetic, inspiring and imaginative leader. His powerful speeches and his careful cultivation of Britain's U.S. allies were vital to the Allies' war effort. After the war's end Churchill was defeated in a general election, but he later became prime minister again in 1951.

De Gaulle, Charles

French statesman. French army officer De Gaulle escaped to London after the German invasion of France in 1939 and set up the Free French to oppose the Vichy regime's collaboration with Germany. Under De Gaulle's leadership, the Free French grew to include some 300,000 fighters, including partisans of the French Resistance. In 1945 he was elected president of France and later founded the Fifth Republic.

Eisenhower, Dwight D.

U.S. general. Eisenhower was part of the U.S. war plans division when he was promoted in June 1942 to become commander of U.S. forces in Europe. He led the Allied landings in North Africa and Sicily and the capture of Rome. As supreme commander of Allied forces, he led the D-Day landings in northern France and the liberation of Paris and advance into Germany. His popularity was reflected by his election in 1952 as the 34th president of the United States, a position he held for 12 years.

Goebbels, Joseph

Nazi leader. Joseph Goebbels was the head of Nazi Party propaganda and later became minister of propaganda in the Nazi government. He used mass media and cinema skilfully to promote Nazi views. At the end of the war, he killed his children and committed suicide with his wife.

Hirohito

Emperor of Japan. Hirohito reluctantly approved the growth of army power and the militarization of Japanese society. He also backed the aggressive foreign policy that eventually led to war, but in 1945 he supported the leaders who wanted to surrender unconditionally. After the war he gave up his divine status and became a constitutional monarch.

Hitler, Adolf

Dictator of Germany. After serving as a soldier in World War I, Adolf Hitler joined a minor political party that he renamed the National Socialist Workers' Party (Nazis). Hitler was elected as chancellor of Germany in 1933 and became leader (Führer) in 1934. His policies were based on anti-Semitism and anti-communism, militarism and the aggressive expansion of Germany. His invasion of Poland in September 1939 sparked the outbreak of the war. Hitler's war leadership was erratic and contributed to Germany's eventual defeat; Hitler himself committed suicide in his bunker in Berlin in the last days of the war.

Hope, Bob

U.S. entertainer. Comedian and singer Bob Hope was one of the biggest movie stars at the start of the war. He became famous for his constant tours of U.S. overseas bases to put on shows for service personnel. Having performed similar tours in later wars in Korea, Vietnam and the Persian Gulf, Hope was acknowledged in 1997 by the U.S. Congress as the first 'Honorary Veteran' in U.S. history.

MacArthur, Douglas

U.S. general. A veteran of World War I, MacArthur commanded the defence of the Philippines against Japan in 1941 before becoming supreme Allied commander in the Southwest Pacific. He commanded the U.S. attacks on New Guinea and the Philippines. After the end of the war, he became supreme Allied commander of Japan and oversaw the country's rapid postwar recovery.

Miller, Dorrie

Miller was an African-American seaman who served at Pearl Harbor in December 1941. Although at the time African Americans were only allowed to serve as orderlies, his courage during the Japanese attack earned him the Navy Cross and made him a national hero.

Montgomery, Bernard

British field marshal. Montgomery led the British Eighth Army in North Africa, where it defeated Rommel's Afrika Korps, and then shared joint command of the invasion of Sicily and Italy. He collaborated with U.S. general Eisenhower on planning the D-Day landings in France, where he commanded all land forces; Montgomery went on to command an army group in the advance toward Germany, where he eventually received the German surrender.

Mussolini, Benito

Italian dictator. Mussolini came to power in Italy in 1922 promoting fascism, a political philosophy based on a militaristic form of nationalism. He led attempts to re-create an Italian empire with overseas conquests. Mussolini became Hitler's ally in 1936 and entered the war on the Nazis' side. Italian campaigns went badly in the Balkans and North Africa, however. When the Allies invaded Italy in 1943 Mussolini was sacked by the king; he became president of a puppet German republic in northern Italy. He was executed by Italian partisan fighters at the end of the war.

Rommel, Erwin

German field marshal. Rommel was a tank commander who led the Afrika Korps in North Africa and later led the defence of northern France against the Allied invasion. When he was discovered to be part of a plot to assassinate Adolf Hitler, he was forced to commit suicide.

Roosevelt, Franklin D.

U.S. president. Democrat politician Franklin Delano Roosevelt enjoyed a privileged upbringing before entering politics and becoming governor of New York. He first came to power as president in 1932, when he was elected to apply his New Deal to solve the worst problems of the Great Depression. Reelected in 1936 and again in 1940 he fully supported the Allies, offering supplies to help fight the Germans. He was reelected in 1944, the only president to be elected for four terms, but died in office shortly before the end of the war against Japan.

Rosie the Riveter

A fictional American worker who first appeared in a popular song but whose image then appeared on posters and stamps to encourage women to take industrial jobs during the war. The various depictions of Rosie were based on a number of specific individual workers.

Stalin, Joseph

Soviet dictator. Stalin was a Bolshevik from Georgia who rose to prominence for his skill as an administrator. In 1922 he became general secretary of the Communist Party of the Soviet Union founded by Lenin. Stalin introduced programs to encourage agriculture and industry and in the 1930s got rid of many thousands of potential enemies in purges, having them jailed or executed. Having made a pact with Hitler in 1939, he was surprised when Hitler invaded the Soviet Union in 1941 but rallied the Red Army to eventual victory. At the end of the war, he imposed Soviet rule on eastern Europe.

Yamamoto, Isoroko

Japanese admiral. Yamamoto was a visionary naval planner who planned Japan's attack on the U.S. base at Pearl Harbor and its early Pacific campaigns. He was killed when the Americans shot down his aircraft in 1943, alerted by decoded Japanese radio communications.

Glossary

Allies One of the two groups of combatants in the war. The main Allies were Britain, the Soviet Union, the United States, British Empire troops, and free forces from occupied nations.

antibiotic A medicine that can halt the spread of infection.

anti-Semitism A hatred of Jews and Judaism.

armistice A temporary halt in fighting agreed to by both sides.

armour A term referring to armoured vehicles, such as tanks.

artillery Large weapons such as big guns and howitzers.

Aryan In Nazi propaganda, relating to a mythical master race of Nordic peoples.

Axis One of the two groups of combatants in the war. The leading Axis powers were Germany, Italy, and Japan.

blitzkrieg A German word meaning "lightning war." It referred to the tactic of rapid land advance supported by great airpower.

Bolsheviks Members of the Communist Party that took power in Russia after the 1917 Revolution.

casualty Someone who is killed or wounded in conflict, or who is missing but probably dead.

collaborator Someone who works with members of enemy forces who are occupying his or her country.

communism A political philosophy based on state control of the economy and distribution of wealth, followed in the Soviet Union from 1917 and in China from 1948.

corps A military formation smaller than an army, made up of a number of divisions operating together under a general.

counteroffensive A set of attacks that defend against enemy attacks.

empire A number of countries governed by a single country.

embargo An order to temporarily stop something, especially trading.

espionage The use of spies or secret agents to obtain information about the plans of a foreign government.

evacuation The act of moving someone from danger to a safe position.

Fascism A political philosophy promoted by Mussolini in Italy based on dictatorial leadership, nationalism and the importance of the state over the individual.

garrison A group of troops placed to defend a location.

Holocaust The systematic German campaign to exterminate millions of Jews and others.

hygiene Following practices, such as keeping clean, that support the maintenance of good health.

independence The state of self-government for a people or nation.

infantry Soldiers who are trained to fight on foot, or in vehicles.

kamikaze Japanese for "divine wind"; the name refers to Japan's suicide pilots.

landing craft Shallow-bottomed boats designed to carry troops and supplies from ships to the shore.

Marine A soldier who serves in close association with naval forces.

materiel A word that describes all the equipment and supplies used by military forces.

morale A sense of common purpose and positive spirits among a group of people or a whole population

occupation The seizure and control of an area by military force.

offensive A planned military attack.

patriotism A love for and promotion of one's country.

propaganda Material such as images, broadcasts or writings that aims to influence the ideas or behaviour of a group of people.

rationing A system of limiting food and other supplies to ensure that everyone gets a similar amount.

reconnaissance A small-scale survey of enemy territory to gather information.

resources Natural materials that are the basis of economic wealth, such as oil, rubber, and agricultural produce.

strategy A detailed plan for achieving success.

strongpoint Any defensive position that has been strengthened to withstand an attack.

siege A military blockade of a place, such as a city, to force it to surrender.

taxes Fees on earnings or financial transactions used by governments to raise money from their citizens.

troops Groups of soldiers.

war bonds A form of investment used by governments in wartime to raise money from savers.

Further Reading

Books

Adams, Simon. *Occupation and Resistance* (Documenting World War II). Wayland, 2008.

Black, Hermann. *World War II, 1939–1945* (Wars Day-by-Day). Brown Bear Reference, 2008.

The Blitz. World War II Replica Memorabilia Pack. Resources for Teaching, 2010.

Burgan, Michael. *America in World War II* (Wars That Changed American History). World Almanac Library, 2006.

Cross, Vince. *Blitz: a Wartime Girl's Diary, 1940–1941* (My Story). Scholastic, 2008.

Deary, Terry, and Mike Phillips. *The Blitz* (Horrible Histories Handbooks). Scholastic 2009.

Dowswell, Paul. *Usborne Introduction to the Second World War.* Usborne Publishing Ltd., 2005.

Gardiner, Juliet. *The Children's War: The Second World War Through the Eyes of the Children of Britain.* Portrait, 2005.

Heppelwhite, Peter. *An Evacuee's Journey* (History Journeys). Wayland, 2004.

Hosch, William L. *World War II: People, Politics and Power* (America at War). Rosen Education Service, 2009.

MacDonald, Fiona. *World War II: Life on the Home Front: A Primary Source History* (In Their Own Words). Gareth Stevens Publishing, 2009.

McNeese, Tim. *World War II: 1939–1945* (Discovering U.S. History). Chelsea House Publishers, 2010.

O'Shei, Tim. *World War II Spies.* Edge Books, 2008.

Price, Sean. *Rosie the Riveter: Women in World War II.* Raintree, 2008.

Price, Sean. *The Art of War: The Posters of World War II* (American History Through Primary Sources). Raintree, 2008.

Ross, Stuart. *The Blitz* (At Home in World War II). Evans Brothers, 2007.

Ross, Stuart. *Evacuation* (At Home in World War II). Evans Brothers, 2007.

Ross, Stuart. *Rationing* (At Home in World War II). Evans Brothers, 2007.

Tonge, Neil. *The Rise of the Nazis* (Documentary World War II). Wayland, 2008.

Wagner, Melissa, and Dan Bryant. *The Big Book of World War II: Fascinating Facts about World War II Including Maps, Historic Photographs and Timelines.* Perseus Books, 2009.

World War II (10 volumes). Grolier Educational, 2006.

World War II (Eyewitness). Dorling Kindersley, 2007.

Websites

www.bbc.co.uk/history/worldwars/wwtwo/
Causes, events and people of the war.

http://www.bbc.co.uk/schools/primaryhistory/world_war2/
Interactive information on what it was like to be a child during the war.

http://www.spartacus.schoolnet.co.uk/2WW.htm
Spartacus Education site on the war.

http://www.nationalarchives.gov.uk/education/worldwar2/
U.S. National Archives primary sources on the war.

http://www.historylearningsite.co.uk/WORLD%20WAR%20TWO.htm
History Learning Site guide to the war.

http://www.telegraph.co.uk/news/newstopics/world-war-2/
Daily Telegraph archive of articles from wartime and from the 70th anniversary of its outbreak.

www.war-experience.org
The Second World War Experience Centre.

www.ibiblio.org/pha
A collection of primary World War II source materials.

www.worldwar-2.net
Complete World War II day-by-day timeline.

http://www.iwm.org.uk/searchlight/server.php?change=SearchlightGalleryView&changeNav=home
Imperial War Museum, London, guide to collections.

Index

Numbers in **bold** refer to illustrations.